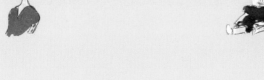

Art isn't work, it's play!

Fred Forster

GETTING CARRIED AWAY

This book was prepared for publication at
Glyph Publishing Arts, San Francisco

Project staff:

Designer
Deanne Delbridge

Book Production
Elizabeth Stein, Will Taylor

Production assistants
Melissa Dimon, Lily B. Williams

Writers
Deanne Delbridge, Lisa Carlson, Lynn Park

Library of Congress Cataloging-in-Publication Data
Forster, Fred
Fred Forster: Getting Carried Away / by Fred Forster

ISBN 0-9714450-0-1

Printed in Korea

Published by
Forbach, Inc., 390 Eucalyptus Ave., Hillsborough, CA 94010
www.gettingcarriedaway.net

Dedicated to my vivacious wife Victoria who
inspired the creation of this book and was
responsible for both herself and me
'Getting Carried Away.'

About the Artist

"People ask me what I do? I drink

beer, I chase women, I play rugby,

I jig, I amble. God has given me

one face and I give myself another.

I make things happen; they don't

happen to me. My favorite quote is:

"One crowded hour of glorious life

is worth an age without a name."

Fred Forster's artistic nature engages on every level of his life. His office overflows with myriad eccentricities: a piano, a harmonica, a Waterford crystal rugby ball and a book entitled *The Leadership Secrets of Attila the Hun.* "I just use it to scare people," Fred says.

He's been known to wear an all-white tuxedo, complete with top hat, when he dresses as a chauffeur to drive his wife around in his white 1964 Rolls Royce. And what is their usual destination…a cowboy bar they've never been to before. When he discovered too many Fred Forsters in the San Francisco phone book, he had himself listed as Fearless Fred, "so no one will be confused as to whom they're calling."

Full of quirky surprises, during a business meeting Fred leaned back and put his feet up on the desk to reveal mismatched Santa Claus socks…in July! When lunch came Fred pulled out a telescoping fork from his desk, a favorite item purchased from a magic shop, and demonstrated how he can reach across and steal his astonished clients' food.

Further examination of his desk yields a drawer filled only with dozens of pairs of reading glasses. ("I'm always losing them!") Where one normally finds office supplies another drawer contains two cookies, some viagra pills (for his friends), scorecards on how to evaluate a woman, one dollar bills with Fred's picture on them, a Tiffany's box with cufflinks in it, and several pieces of candy.

What makes his wild spirit seem doubly so is that Fred's art flourishes amidst the bustle and stress of big business. "He can be on the phone turning a multi-million dollar deal and be writing a limerick at the same time," says friend Ed Marr. "He was proficient at multi-tasking long before multi-tasking was in vogue."

Even his 1994 marriage to Victoria was an art event. Staged during half-time at an invitational rugby match at Stanford in which Fred participated, the ceremony included players from all over the world. Fred, who quickly changed from his grimy jersey into a white tux, walked onto the field followed by a bagpipe player to meet his bride. She and her father arrived in the Rolls Royce and a condensed version of the entire spectacle was broadcast world-wide on the Sports Channel.

Expressing his sardonic humor through drawing and painting seemed inevitable. Not playing at being something other than what they are, his collection of naïve or "self-taught" art presented here depicts scenes drawn from his personal life experiences. His storytelling artwork is often sprinkled with recurring iconography: a banana (his favorite food), a man fishing who never catches anything, ("the part of me that wants to sit back and watch the world go by," says Fred).

Infused with joy and mystery, playfulness and depth, the body of work assembled in this book celebrates a man loved for his wit whose spirit inspires us all!

Fred has played sports since he was ten. A natural athlete with a need to win, at sixteen he crossed the finish line first as a sprinter in an Irish hundred yard dash.

"Bill, in the drawing, is actually a kicker on my rugby team," says Fred. "He has played with me on the old boy rugby teams: the San Francisco Señors and the California Bald Eagles."

"Bill runs very, very slowly. You can see he's back with the turtle while I'm out in front."

Forster was included as one of seven to play an 'invitation only' young man's rugby tournament in Switzerland in 2001. With the same passion that has driven him to compete world-wide, he once flew to Argentina to watch sixteen consecutive games in the world cup seven-aside rugby finals and to Australia to see the famous Lions play the Aussie world champions.

"I'm one of the few living artists who can say I've had a picture hung in the Louvre!" It was 1984 when Fred did his first drawing while at his farm in northern California. "I sat down and decided to draw everything I could see around me that began with a 'B'. I drew a banana, a barn, a beer can and a brown cow. I called it Multiple Objects."

Feeling an immediate desire to be recognized by the most venerated institution of classical art, Forster stuffed his small drawing in his raincoat pocket and hopped a plane to Paris where his daughter was living. With electrician's tape he carefully mounted it over a framed print on the wall in the Louvre and had his daughter document the proud moment with a rare and memorable photograph.

"I was thinking of things that are BIG. What's the BIG PICTURE? So I drew a Big Mac, a big head, the Big Dipper and so on," explains Fred. This idea of 'different but related objects' became 'different but related experiences' in later paintings such as 'Minor Mishaps', showing a high heel caught in a grate and a painter spilling his bucket of paint. The concept of different but related ideas evolved even further in 1988 and 1990 when 'Scenes Seldom Seen' and 'Ways of the World' became real-life dreamscapes that beg the question: have I actually seen this before or just imagined it?

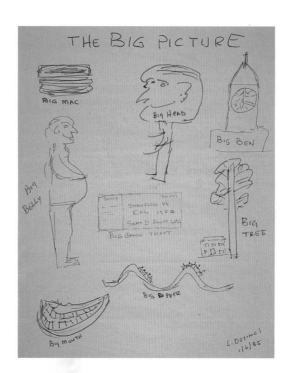

A farmer went up in a balloon one day. Clouds drifted in and he floated on and on. The clouds cleared and he saw a guy down in the field and maneuvered down to him. The farmer shouted, "Where are we?" and the guy ignored him. And the farmer said again, "Where are we?" and the guy ignored him again.

The farmer started drifting away when he called once more, "Where are we?" and the guy below said, "You're in a balloon."

The farmer said, "I bet that guy down there is a lawyer because he didn't answer my call the first time and when he did answer, he told me something I knew before I even asked the question."

"Do you know how to catch a polar bear? You go up north and find a frozen lake with a big rock beside it. Then you go out a little bit onto the ice and cut a hole in it. You take a packet of frozen peas and you put one pea every six inches around the hole. Then you hide behind the rock and when the bear comes for a pea, you kick him in the ice hole."

"I remembered this story being passed around from the time I was working as an engineer with Bechtel Corporation and later decided to do a drawing of it," recounts Forster. "In those days I was churning out drawings on newsprint. Later, when I bought more expensive paper I had to spend a longer time on them because otherwise I would be wasting the paper."

"I signed them 'L. DeVinci' purposely misspelled so that people wouldn't get our drawings mixed up. Then I changed the signature to 'Fred' or 'F. Forster' or 'Fred F.' or 'Fearless Fred' because I didn't want daVinci to get all the credit."

Fred's creative spirit rages outside the boundaries, spilling over in all directions, manifesting itself in everything from eclectic office attire to putting up jams, to jamming on his trumpet at night in a field, his farm donkeys following him one by one in a line like the Pied Piper.

He also plays to them (from his porch) on the piano, the bagpipes, harmonica, accordion, and Irish flute. "But the trumpet is clearly their favorite," says Fred. "They're well-educated asses."

Forster originally adopted the donkeys from the U.S. Bureau of Land Management because he needed lawn mowers for his 10-acre farm. "It worked so well I kept breeding them. Now I have nine lovers of 'a little night music'."

The serene setting, which includes a private lake and rich farmland, yields a yearly crop of apples, almonds, and apricots which Fred promptly puts up in jars as jam and distributes with gusto to friends, family, and clients. Although the wooded grounds provide inspiration for many of his landscapes, it is the animals who more often give life to his wry mythologies. 'The Other Side of the Fence' and 'High Hopes' are two examples of the way Forster observes everyday rural life and finds the metaphor within.

COLOR PLATES

Give Me A Home

1987

This one is a picture of all these buffalo roaming and some of them are jumping over fences. There's one buffalo sitting down inside the fence there, and he's saying "Some days you just don't feel like roaming." I suppose everybody needs a break from what they're doing once in awhile. You know that song "Give me a home where the buffalo roam, where the deer and the antelope play." In this case, they're playing chess.

High Hopes

1989

Coming down from the farm one day I saw a goat up on a sheep's back eating apples off a tree. So I put three sheep and a goat in the drawing with a monkey throwing a rock at the sheep trying to get the sheep to jump so that the goat would fall down. They're all trying to torpedo the goat.

First Class Ass

1987

In Ireland when I was a kid there were no cars on the road. There were just asses with carts and horses with carts. The poorer people had asses. This guy here, he's got two milk churns on the cart. They used to milk the cows and put the milk in churns and haul it to the creamery on an ass and cart. Sometimes if a farmer got too drunk to go home, the bartender would put him on the cart and turn the ass loose and the ass would walk home, as he knew where to go. These were first class asses—they're very intelligent animals.

Going Bananas
1988

My friend had a car, a checker cab, so I drew a picture of the checker cab and then decided to fill it up with monkeys. They all have bananas and there are banana trees around. One monkey holds a French flag and one blows a horn. And there's a sign on the trunk saying, "We want bananas," and then there's a McDonald's, and a little elephant walking, and the black man's fishing.

GOING BANANAS

FEARLESS FRED   OCT 10-1988

Ways of the World

1990

One is "Wrong Way"—the guy's sitting backwards on a horse. Then there's a monkey with a football that says "No Way"—he's not going to succeed. The next one is a street and it says "One Way" but the title is "Another Way" because the runner is going the opposite way. Then there's a guy hammering in a nail, but he's got the *head* of the nail facing in instead of the front of it; that's called the "Hard Way." Then there's a pregnant woman, and it says "My Way." She got him to marry her by getting pregnant. The next one is a guy in a boat pouring a glass of wine, and it says "Any Way"—he's going to do it anyway. The guy on the hammock is doing it the "Easy Way"'. Then there's a guy boxing a polar bear, that's "A Strange Way." Then a turtle racing against a hare, it's called a "Fast Way."

Prize Fighters
1990

Two women were fighting over me. They both wanted to leave me and they both wanted to stay with me. One was willing to stay with me unconditionally, and the other thought I was the best man in the world, except for a few little quirks that needed to be straightened out. She tried to change me and then she gave up and left. I guess the prize fighters represent the two women and I must be the prize.

PRIZE FIGHTERS

FEARLESS FRED   July 22 – 1990

Multiple Bounce
1987

I had some Australians visiting me at the time. There's a kangaroo, and he's on a pogo stick and this pogo stick is on a trampoline…so he's really bouncing. Then I put a fat lady bouncing on the trampoline too. This painting is replete with categories of beings that bounce so I must have been feeling pretty bouncy at the time. I always have a man fishing in the background. This time he finally caught something.

Stuck Truck
1989

I saw a truck with the back wheel stuck in the mud like that and I was wondering how they'd get it out. I figured out how *I* would do it.

STUCK TRUCK

7/24/89

Horse Sense

1988

You can see that there's a fence and all the animals are either going over the fence or through the fence—except for the horse that's going through a gate in the fence. It may sound simple, but a lot of people spend their lives crashing through fences that don't really exist. There are gates there that could be just easily walked through.

HORSE SENSE

FEARLESS FRED
4-29-88

Sheep Kicker

1997

Where I live in Ireland there's a place where they let the sheep run wild and they get out on the roads. Sometimes when you're driving, the sheep lie down in the road, and I have to stop the car. Then I have to get out and try to kick the sheep, but the problem is, the sheep don't stand around. As soon as you get out of the car they run away. So it's a hard job to get out there and kick them—you have to run like crazy.

Medical Melody
1989

A man is going for an operation, and instead of having a chemical anesthetic, all the doctors are singing him to sleep. You see them all there—some of them with violins, and there's a monkey underneath the bed playing a tune on a horn. The idea here is that he'll just go to sleep soon. He's drinking a beer too. It's a form of anesthetic. It anesthetizes people from their everyday chores and life.

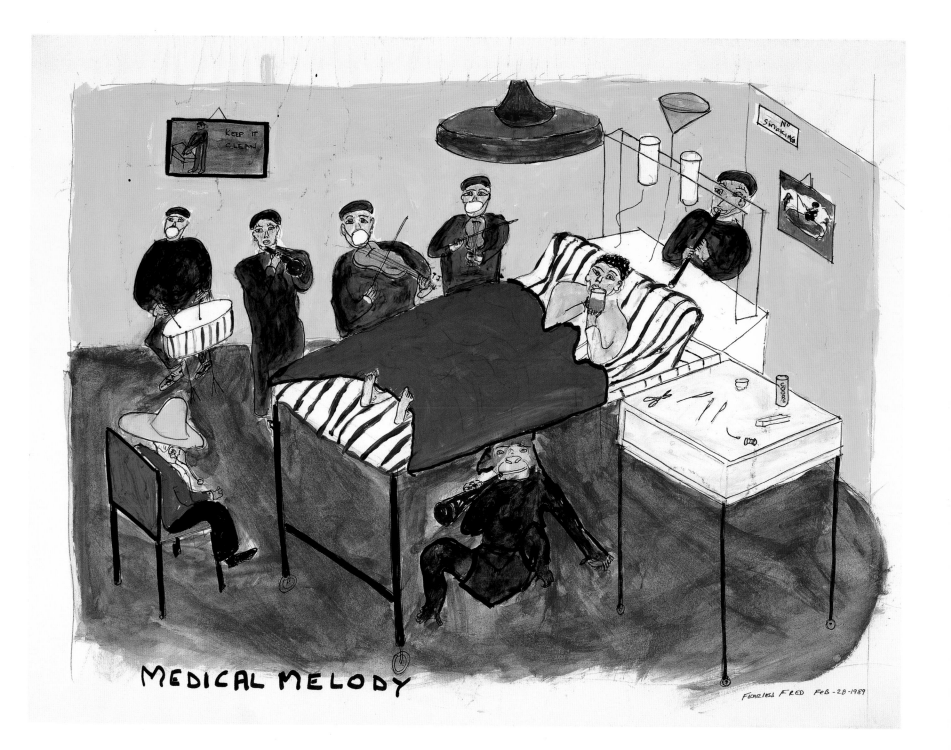

MEDICAL MELODY

Fearless Fred Feb-28-1989

Teaser
1991

There's a poem called *Albert and the Lion* in which this young guy named Albert was taken to the zoo by his parents. The lion was sitting there, quiet and docile, and this was not Albert's image of the lion; he thought lions were supposed to be ferocious and wild. So Albert got his stick with the horse's head handle and shoved it in the lion's ear (that's part of the poem). The lion pulled Albert inside the cage with him and swallowed him whole.

TEASER

FEARLESS FRED Aug-25-1991

Horse of a Different Color
1987

I was in this bar in Cool, California when a horse walked in and they started giving it beer. They had TV cameras in there and I was wondering what was going on and they said, "Oh this horse just won." He just finished winning a hundred-mile race from Tahoe to Cool. So I drew him standing up at the bar. The horse is red, white and blue. You'd never see a horse that color if you were sober.

Getting Carried Away

1990

I got a picture of a coach like the queen rides in and I drew the coach, but instead of horses, I put some asses pulling it. That was about the time I met my wife, Victoria. I met her in October 1989 so it was the first picture I drew after that and subconsciously I was "Getting Carried Away", so I drew a picture of me in the coach. There are monkeys with the adios signs up there with all the other women—they're all waving goodbye to me. They all knew (except me) that I was getting carried away.

GETTING CARRIED AWAY

FEARLESS FRED   4-22-1990

Catchers
1988

I only put dog catchers in there at first. I had this van and three people running after dogs. And then I decided it needed more, so I put other catchers in there. Maybe someone was trying to catch *me*. There's a policeman catching a thief; there's a bride catching a husband; there's a guy catching fish in the background and a trapeze artist catching another guy. This is a very catching picture.

Fast Ass
1989

You remember Lady Godiva who was famous for getting votes for women? That's why she rode naked through the streets. She was protesting that women weren't allowed to vote. When I originally drew this picture, I was drawing Lady Godiva, and that's what I was going to call it. Then I drew a monkey riding an ass who was winning the race. The monkey has a stick with a carrot on it holding it out in front of the ass to make the ass run.

Sour Note

1988

That's a picture of an orchestra and the conductor has a gun under the podium. One of the fiddlers played a bad note, so he shot him. That's why it's called "Sour Note". There's a guy fishing in the picture on the wall. And there's a Mexican sitting way at the back…observing. And there's Sam playing the piano. The fiddler has played his last sour note.

Change of Heart

1989

Once I knew this woman who said she never wanted to get married but kept saying she wanted to live with me. She was not being honest. She obviously *did* want to get married. But then she said, "F--- you. I'm leaving." She had a change of heart.

Round Trip

1988

I was in a restaurant one day and there were round tables, but the waiter kept whizzing by me—he was a well-trained waiter. He avoided eye contact at all times. The only way I could attract his attention was to stick my foot out so he'd trip over it. It shows him spilling the wine on that lady's dress. The picture of United Airlines is advertising roundtrips on the wall.

ROUND TRIP

FEARLESS FRED
4-4-1988

The Other Side of the Fence
1987

I was coming back from the farm one day and I saw this cow with her head stuck through the fence and she couldn't get back. So I got out of the car and tried to get the cow's head back in and she just started jerking and jerking. See the grass? It's greener on the other side. People do things to get what they think is greener even though it really isn't. That's why she stuck her head through the fence.

THE OTHERSIDE
OF THE FENCE

FRED F.
5-23-1987

Blunder Bus
1987

It's a bus for people who blunder…There are two men pushing a busload of monkeys up a hill. It's also being towed by a Mexican riding an ass. They're going to the zoo, but the bus broke down. There's a Mexican looking over the fence. There are banana skins along the way, so one of the guys—when he pushes the bus—is going to slip on the banana skin.

Minor Mishaps
1988

This has eight different things going on. They're all little things that can happen to people that can be a source of great annoyance. Right in the center there is a lady with her high heel stuck in a grate. The jogger has the dog running up and biting him on the ass. Joggers are always afraid of dogs. There's an older woman with a flat tire, and she's wondering what the hell to do—can't change the tire herself. There's a guy trying to do log-rolling and he's falling off the log.

MINOR
MIS HAPS

FEARLESS FRED
Aug 21 - 1988

Play it Again, Sam
1991

Remember the movie *Casablanca*? It looks like Humphrey Bogart is forcing him to play it because Sam was saying in that movie, "No I don't want to play it." And Humphrey said, "Play it, Sam."—he never really said "Play it again, Sam." One of my lady friends had left me and she wanted to come back and another one wanted to come into my life and I just wanted a time out. I was going out with a third woman by then— playing the field.

Asses & Apes
1988

I have some asses with monkeys on their backs riding around the roads and going wild around the country and jumping over fences. See the big gorilla right here in front? Then I've got one ass with two apes on his back. One monkey is riding with his hands up and is satisfied with his objectives in life. He throws his hands up. I don't know what the monkeys symbolize, but some people used to say monkeys represent the will of God in mythology.

ASSES AND APES

FEARLESS FRED JUNE 19 - 1988

Right of Way
1988

That's a picture of a cow lying on a railroad track, and the cow refuses to move. And the conductor is out trying to beat the cow with a stick and the driver is standing on the train with a gun but the gun won't do him any good because if he shoots the cow he still won't get the cow off the track. There's a monkey swinging off the branch of the tree enjoying it all and a couple of asses grazing in the field behind. The train has the right of way but the cow won't yield.

RIGHT OF WAY

FEARLESS FRED
MARCH 5-1988

Sumotime

1991

The title was originally going to be "Summertime" like the song. "Summertime, and the livin is easy, fish is jumpin' and the cotton is high." See in the background there's a guy bringing cotton in from the cotton field. There's a black man fishing and the fish is jumpin'. There is a guy lying on the hammock—livin' is easy—a case of Coors beer, a guy making hamburgers, and the Mexican is playing a violin. When I'd done all that, there was a big gap in the middle, so I decided to put in Sumo wrestlers. So I changed it to 'Sumotime'.

Ass Power
1990

A broken down Rolls Royce is being towed by this guy riding two assess through the streets of Manhattan. There are all kinds of stores and things and a monkey climbing out of a manhole. There's a travel agency, a gun shop, and Trump Tower. There's a pet shop and a Mexican with a Coors. There's an art store and inside the art store there's a picture, and in that picture there's a black man fishing. There's a policeman standing at the corner wondering what's going on. That's a stray dog, by the way. He's got nothing to do with the Mexican.

FEARLESS FRED   July 8 - 1990

Music Man
1992

It's got a bit of everything in it. It's got the yellow brick road coming from the Oz castle going to a stadium. It has *Hello Dolly* on the right. It has a homosexual Indian wearing pink pants. It's got a Japanese tourist with no film in his camera. It has a sailor on 24 hours' leave with his girlfriend. And there's a statue of the Flat Earth Society next to the sailor; the world is flat and it has Ireland in the center of the world. Then it has the *Music Man* right in the center near the building. It has a band coming down the street after him and five or six chorus girls doing a dance and the Wells Fargo wagon is ahead of that.

Scenes Seldom Seen

1988

This painting is about things you can imagine seeing, but you never really see them. Like there's a nun kicking a field goal—but you never really see that. There's a chimney sweep with a bride. It used to be considered good luck for a bride to kiss a chimney sweep just after she got married. But those days are gone. It was traditional in Ireland back at the turn of the century. You'd have a chimney sweep show up outside the church. But you never see that anymore. And that's a royal flush— a poker hand—the best poker hand you can get. Nobody's ever seen one. And there's a nice can of Coors there and a skier skiing around a banana tree. You'd seldom see a banana tree up on the ski slopes. And you never see an elephant doing a jump over a wall like a horse. The last one is Newton discovering the law of gravity when he sat under a tree and an apple fell on his head, and he said, "I know what I've discovered: the law of gravity." But you never see someone sitting under an apple tree with an apple falling on their head.

SCENES SELDOM SEEN

FEARLESS FRED Oct 24-1988

Dangerous Dan McGrew

1988

There's a poem by Robert Service called *The Shooting of Dan McGrew* about a miner who came into the Malamute Saloon in Fairbanks, Alaska. Dangerous Dan McGrew was in a solo game, not poker. He's the guy in the yellow shirt. Lou is the woman who left the miner to go out with Dan McGrew. She was the cause of all the trouble. There's Dan McGrew and the miner shooting at each other. I had a big gap in the center so I decided just to put a monkey there eating a banana.

DANGEROUS DAN McGREW

Footwork
1988

You know Houdini could do the same things with his feet as he could with his hands. He could tie knots. It's monkeys doing the soft shoe and one playing the piano with his feet. I tried playing the piano with my toes like that and I couldn't quite get a tune, but I could pick off notes.

Poor Sports

1995

Various scenes in this picture show how some people will stop at nothing to win and are often sore losers. Like hitting your opponent with a tennis racket, blindfolding a horse in a race, or pulling your opponent back.

POOR SPORTS

FRED FORSTER MARCH 5th 1995

Hauling Asses

1990

I had gotten two asses from the government up at the farm and they had a baby ass. One day the asses escaped and went down to another farm. I went down with my son Danny and my niece Sarah to round up the asses and bring them back. I didn't quite know how to control the asses at the time. We put halters on them and put the rope around the bumper of the car. The asses were going at different speeds because of their sizes. I was trying to keep an average speed up but Jack was getting ahead. He was bigger. Marguerite was at the right speed, and the baby ass, Solomon, was too slow, so there was Sarah pushing him along. All the neighbors came out looking at us and thought this was a great sight—they'd never seen anybody "haulin' ass" before.

Passover

1991

There are two different Passovers here. There's one of a football player passing a ball over an overpass. Then below that there's a Jewish Passover. There's a bunch of pink elephants up on the bridge. See the car there with two naked ladies? One day I was downtown and this lady called me and said, "Would you like to go for a drink?" and she showed up with two of them in a limo with the top off (open sun roof) and took me on a tour of the bars.

Roll Playing
1997

At the Plaza Hotel in New York, in the Palm Court, they had a piano player. A guy is throwing bread rolls at the piano player and the maitre d' is trying to hit the guy on the head to stop him from throwing rolls. There's another rugby player over here, probably me, also throwing rolls at the piano player.

Aces & Eights

1987

As the story is told, Wild Bill Hickock was playing poker and somebody thought he was cheating, so they shot him. He had aces and eights in his hand. I like playing poker so I just decided I could win with aces and eight's—it's a winning hand. I had Tony Nardoni living with me at the time. He posed for all these pictures. You can tell by the woman lying on the couch, she looks like a man because of Tony's figure.

ACES AND 8's

F FORSTER
9-27-1987

Coming to America
1993

A big boat is approaching the shore, and there's a couple of monkeys trying to climb on board, and there are some water skiers and a circus up to the left. There's a big church and a band and a Motel 6. And outside the motel there's a bunch of Rolls Royce cars. And then there's the Ritz Carlton and they have asses parked outside—so the poorer people are staying at the Ritz and the richer people are staying at Motel 6. It means people in America can do what they feel like.

COMING TO
AMERICA

FEARLESS FRED   April 1993

Cake Walk

1990

This is in Coloma, California down by the American River. I was out river rafting one day and I got back and pulled into this restaurant and bar. I was going to just get into some clothes and go in and have a few drinks. This car pulled up, a woman and her daughter got out of it and one of them had a big birthday cake in her hands. She put the cake down on the trunk of the car and turned around to do something and when she did the cake slipped off the car and landed facedown on the gravel. As it was falling, she tried to grab it with her hands so she got that gucky cream all over her hands. I was just getting out of the car at that time and I had a damp towel in my hands. I was going to say to her, "Well you can't have your cake and eat it too", but I thought she would have probably hit me over the head so instead I offered her the towel to wipe her hands off. The poor woman was so fed up—a real nice big cake—obviously for a big birthday or wedding.

CAKE WALK

FEARLESS FRED   9/3/90

Ships That Pass in the Night

1987

Now this is not typical of my drawings at all. There doesn't seem to be any humor in it. I wasn't even going to put my name on this one. It doesn't have the Mexican; it doesn't have a black man fishing. It has the Titanic about to hit an iceberg. This was done on Christmas day 1987, a couple of years after my first wife left.

SHIPS THAT PASS IN THE NIGHT

F Forster
12-25-87

Life in the Fast Lane
1988

It has two lanes in the picture—a fast lane and a slow lane. There's a Mexican and a bunch of asses in the slow lane on the right, but in the left lane there are cars running over people. I was doing a lot of business at that time; there were a lot of sharks around trying to screw me out of things. A lot of business people are like that—they're money-hungry, running people over, mowing them down, doesn't bother them, as long as they get their money. There are people running across the road and guys lying in holes and there are two hitchhikers, and a horse galloping down the road. And there's a sign saying, 'Keep up speed,' and a police car waiting to trap them all. It's all treachery stuff—all things you've got to be alert to. The two women hitchhikers with a bottle of whiskey, for instance.

LIFE IN THE FAST LANE

FEARLESS FRED
JUNE 5ᵗʰ 1988

Skaters

2000

This has an elephant pulling a sleigh. Santa Claus is coming to town, and it has the Wicked Witch of the West with a gun trying to shoot Santa Claus. Then it has another skater trying to go past him, and a Scotsman with a drum, but instead of marching, he's skating. Maybe it's a lot of mixed up things that don't really add up to anything. And the Mexican is riding a bicycle—this is a frozen ice road. The odd thing about this picture is that I never sketched it; I just painted it. I draw all my pictures with pencil or pen first, but this one had no outline.

Down Beat
1989

Downbeat shows three musicians playing a tune. One with a trumpet, one with a violin, and one with a bass. If they do something wrong, then these people behind them are going to bang them on the head— one with a washboard, one a chair, and one with a tennis racket—so they have to watch their notes.

Unfinished Symphony

2000

I deliberately didn't finish it because I couldn't find a way of pulling it all together. I probably started off by drawing the Statue of Liberty two or three years ago. Then I said, this thing has been around my house for a year or so, so I drew the Transamerica building and the Golden Gate Bridge. I drew a trumpet, put a computer there and a football player—a whole bunch of miscellany.

Bull Run
1993

I don't know if you've ever been chased by a bull but it can be pretty scary. This guy is about to jump the fence and there's somebody outside there with a horse and buggy. They're just watching the events. He was showing a red flag to the bull…it's his own fault. The guy behind is pulling the bull's tail to keep the bull from chasing him.

BULL RUN

Fearless Fred   1/10/93

Asspenn
1988

I just decided to draw some asses that were serving as ski lifts and the asses would tow the skiers up to the top of the hill. I had to have a way for the asses to come down so the asses came down on toboggans. I figured, well, they have to go into a pen in order to be ready to take up the next skier.

Doubles With Troubles

1988

I play tennis, though I never made it to Wimbledon. They're playing mixed doubles. The black man serving is being tackled by a football player—so that's trouble for him. The woman on the receiving end is being roped by a cowboy with a lasso. There's a guy throwing a rock at the guy in the blue shirt. And the woman in the yellow dress is being poked in the back by the guy in white with a stick. The Mexican's sitting by observing and the black man's fishing in the background. The monkey's watching over the fence.

DOUBLES
WITH
TROUBLES

FEARLESS FRED
AUG 14-1988

Life Begins at 40

2002

This picture was drawn for Joseph Forster who had just had his fortieth birthday party in San Francisco. Several details may tantalize the viewer such as the Golden Gate Bridge and the Statue of Liberty in the same water, a sumo wrestler playing a piano, and the waiter sampling the wine before pouring it. Joe can be seen in the king's uniform while his father Fred, using his long fork, reaches for somebody else's cookies.

LIFE BEGINS AT 40

Church Bound

1992

My business associate was getting married, and I drove his bride to the wedding. The car didn't actually break down, but I was always wondering what would happen if the car did break down. In this picture the Rolls Royce broke down on the way to church, and the bride is out helping to push it, and there's a gas station across the road. The train is coming and the barriers are down, so they have to wait until the train passes. They have to get gas, too, but there's a little sign on the gas station that says it's closed. That guy in the red shirt is the father of the bride. That's me driving, wearing the hat. Nobody's steering though, is there?

Holier than Thou

2000

Now there's an old joke about a guy who goes to the priest and says he wants to baptize his dog, and the priest says, "You're crazy. We don't baptize dogs here." So he says, "Well the Protestant minister is willing to do it for $500." So the priest replies, "Bring the little puppy around and we'll make a good Catholic out of him." I have all these dogs lining up to be baptized except one is a sumo wrestler with a sheep. The dog that's past the font there has a halo on his head—he's turned holy— he's on the other side. This guy, Reverend Barker, has a sign on his van that says, "Dogs baptized $40—Certificates $10 extra."

HOLIER THAN THOU

FEARLESS FRED   10/16/2000

Flying High
1995

I was married in October 1994 on a rugby field at half time. That's the way I was dressed up at the wedding—in a white tuxedo. We flew to the Caribbean for our honeymoon. *Erin Go Bragh* means Ireland forever.